CULTURE IN ACTION

Punk

MUSIC, FASHION, ATTITUDE!

Charlotte Guillain

Chicago, Illinois

www.heinemannraintree.com
Visit our website to find out
more information about
Heinemann-Raintree books.

To order:

☎ Phone 888-454-2279
🖥 Visit www.heinemannraintree.com
to browse our catalog and order online.

© 2011 Raintree
an imprint of Capstone Global Library, LLC
Chicago, Illinois

Visit our website at www.heinemannraintree.com

Edited by Louise Galpine and Diyan Leake
Designed by Victoria Allen
Original illustrations © Capstone Global Library Ltd 2011
Illustrated by Randy Schirz
Picture research by Hannah Taylor

Originated by Capstone Global Library Ltd
Printed in and bound in China by CTPS

14 13 12 11 10
10 9 8 7 6 5 4 3 2 1

Library of Congress Cataloging-in-Publication Data
Guillain, Charlotte.
  Punk : music, fashion, attitude! / Charlotte Guillain.
    p. cm. -- (Culture in action)
  Includes bibliographical references and index.
  ISBN 978-1-4109-3916-6 (hc)
  1. Punk rock music--History and criticism--Juvenile
literature. 2. Punk culture--Juvenile literature. I. Title.
  ML3534.G85 2011
  781.66--dc22
                        2009052585

Acknowledgments
The author and publishers are grateful to the following for
permission to reproduce copyright material: Alamy Images
pp. **12** (© M&N), **18** (© M&N); Corbis pp. **5** (Richard
Olivier), **13** (Bettmann), **14** (Giovanni Giannoni), **23** (Roger
Ressmeyer), **24** (Joe Giron), **27** (Reuters/Eric Thayer);
Getty Images pp. **4** (WireImage/Tom Hill), **6** (Michael Ochs
Archive/Richard McCaffrey), **7** (Redferns/Roberta Bailey),
20 (Popperfoto/Rolls Press), **22** (Redferns/Ebet Roberts);
Lebrecht Music & Arts p. **8** (© Mirrorpix); Photolibrary p. **16**
(James Fraser); Rex Features pp. **9** (Ray Stevenson), **10** (Andre
Csillag), **17** (Eugene Adebari), **19** (Dreadshots), **21** (Nicholas
Bailey), **26** (Brian J. Ritchie).

Cover photograph reproduced with permission of Rex
Features (Peter Stuart).

We would like to thank Patrick Allen and Jackie Murphy for
their invaluable help in the preparation of this book.

Every effort has been made to contact copyright holders
of any material reproduced in this book. Any omissions
will be rectified in subsequent printings if notice is given
to the publisher.

Disclaimer
All the Internet addresses (URLs) given in this book were valid
at the time of going to press. However, due to the dynamic
nature of the Internet, some addresses may have changed, or
sites may have changed or ceased to exist since publication.
While the author and publisher regret any inconvenience this
may cause readers, no responsibility for any such changes can
be accepted by either the author or the publisher.

Author
Charlotte Guillain is an experienced
children's author and editor. Her
favorite punk band is The Clash.

Literacy consultant
Jackie Murphy is Director of Arts at
the Center of Teaching and Learning,
Northeastern Illinois University. She
works with teachers, artists, and
school leaders internationally.

Expert
Patrick Allen is an award-winning
author and music educator, whose
work as an Advanced Skills Teacher
of Music takes him into schools,
colleges, and universities.

Contents

Some words are printed in bold, **like this**. You can find out
what they mean by looking in the glossary on page 30.

What Is Punk?

What do you think when you hear the word "punk"? Do you think of bands you are listening to today? Or does it make you think of music from the past? Does punk make you think of a certain hairstyle or fashion? Or an attitude?

Before punk music, teenagers had found a fresh new life in the **pop** music of the 1950s and 1960s. By the 1970s, however, many rock stars were earning huge amounts of money. Life was often hard for ordinary people, and some young people began to feel they had nothing in common with popular **culture**. Instead they could relate to rebels they saw in movies, who fought against the limits an older **generation** had set in place. Now music was ready for its own rebellion.

"We set our own direction, and we don't follow anyone."—Johnny Rotten

Punk punches pop

Punk rock hit the world in the late 1970s. Most punk musicians had little money or musical training. But they were rebelling against a type of music they hated. They made up their own, new style and taught themselves to play music in a very loud and simple way.

The word "punk"

The word "punk" was an insult in the 1500s. Shakespeare used the word several times in his plays. By the 1600s the word was used to describe rotten wood, and later it meant a troublesome young person. The writer Dave Marsh wrote about "punk rock" for the first time in 1971. The insult became something positive, challenging everything **conservative** and comfortable.

Over time, punk developed so that it was not just about music— it became a whole attitude.

Early Punk

Punk began in different parts of the United States. By 1969 a few bands in the city of Detroit, Michigan, were starting to play a new sound. MC5 and The Stooges played a loud, rebellious kind of music that offered something different from soft **pop** and **disco**.

Drugs

Many punk musicians lived in a wild way that reflected their image. Sadly, some were badly affected by drugs and alcohol, and many famous musicians, such as Iggy Pop, were **addicts**.

New York scene

By 1973 bands that played a new sound were performing at a club called CBGB in New York City. A magazine called *Punk* came out in 1976 with articles about the new music. Young people became interested in the developing scene. Bands such as The New York Dolls, The Ramones, and Blondie started to become popular. All these bands were called "punk" to start with. Later some bands' music was called "**New Wave**," because it was not as hard as punk.

James Osterberg changed his name to Iggy Pop and began singing with The Stooges in 1967. The band members became famous for their wild behavior on stage, which influenced the punk scene that soon followed.

The Ramones

The Ramones came from Queens, New York. These four musicians made up names for themselves, all with the last name Ramone. They set the harder musical style of true punk rock music. Many of their songs last for two minutes or less, with only four **chords**. The message was that anyone could play punk music—you just needed to play a few chords very fast and loud.

Malcolm McLaren (left) ran a clothing store in London with his partner, Vivienne Westwood (right). They stocked clothing that became a big part of the punk look.

Punk in the United Kingdom

Early punk rock soon traveled to the United Kingdom. The British fashion designer Malcolm McLaren visited New York City in 1972 and met The New York Dolls. He became interested in the new sound that they and other bands were blasting out. He took punk back to London, England.

The Godmother of Punk

Patti Smith grew up in New Jersey in the 1950s. Her family was very religious. By the early 1970s, she was friends with many artists and musicians in New York City. Then she formed her own rock band and released the album *Horses* in 1975. This record influenced many punk musicians and earned her the nickname "the Godmother of Punk."

The Sex Pistols

In London, McLaren started to manage a band that later became The Sex Pistols. John Lydon, an art student with green hair, became the singer and changed his name to Johnny Rotten. The band's sound was based on The Ramones, but its look and behavior was new. The Sex Pistols' first concert was in 1975. To shock people, they smashed equipment and started fights at their concerts.

Everything in punk happened in a fast, direct, and rough way. Many bands and fans started their own magazines called **fanzines**. They were usually just black and white photocopies. Many punk bands in the United Kingdom had to find their own concert venues and even started their own **record labels**.

The Sex Pistols acted out the punk values of rebelling against **conventional** music and behavior.

Punk Makes Headlines

The Sex Pistols' first single, "**Anarchy** in the UK," came out in 1976. It was immediately banned from British daytime radio. The **authorities** worried that the song's **lyrics** encouraged young people to rebel against the government. Not long after the single was released, the band members appeared on British television and shocked many viewers with their attitude and language. Many other punk bands formed in the United Kingdom around this time, including The Clash, Siouxsie and the Banshees, and The Buzzcocks.

In the United States, The Ramones recorded their first album in 1976, followed by two more in 1977. Although none of these records reached a very high position on the popular music charts, many people see these albums as among the best punk music ever recorded.

Joe Strummer was the lead singer in The Clash. His real name was John Mellor, but he gave himself his stage name to describe the way he played.

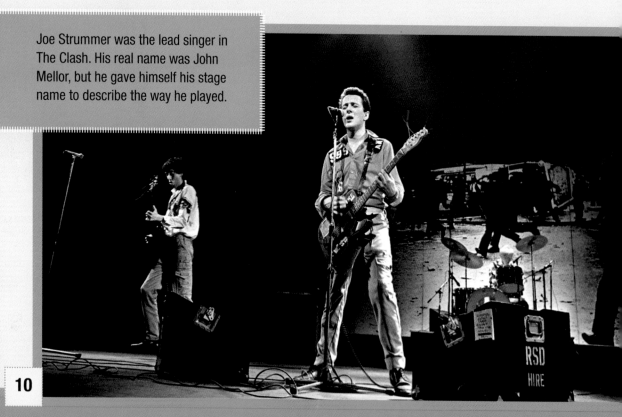

Learn three chords

The great thing about punk music was that anybody could start a band, even if they had never played an instrument before. One punk **fanzine** famously printed pictures of three guitar **chords** and told readers, "This is a chord, this is another, this is a third. Now form a band." Try it yourself!

Steps to follow:

1. With a guitar, learn to play the A chord using this diagram.

2. Now learn to play the D chord.

3. Finally, learn to play the E chord.

4. Practice playing the chords in different orders. Try to play them as fast as you can. You now have the basics of a punk song.

5. Write and perform your own punk song. Will you and your friends form a band?

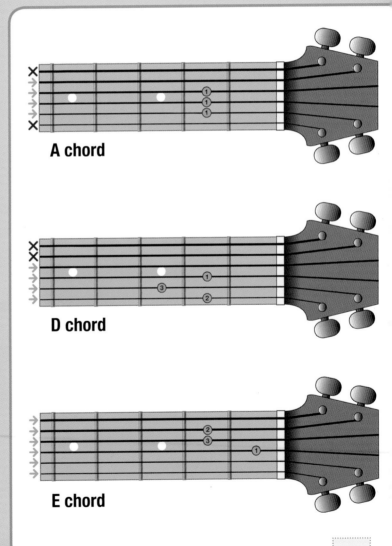

A chord

D chord

E chord

Notorious

By 1977 punk had become **notorious**. The **media** focused on some musicians' outrageous behavior and older people's reactions to punk. One central idea of punk had been to shock people, and this seemed to be working.

The Sex Pistols' **record label** got nervous and decided to drop the band. Then the bass player, Glen Matlock, quit. A fan named Sid Vicious was asked to join the band in his place. Malcolm McLaren said, "If Johnny Rotten is the voice of punk, then Vicious is the attitude." There was a big celebration for Queen Elizabeth II's "Silver Jubilee" (25 years of her reign) in 1977, so The Sex Pistols released the **controversial** single "God Save the Queen." The lyrics were not really supportive of the royal family. Again, the song was banned by many radio stations.

The cover for the single "God Save the Queen" was shocking to many people who were used to respecting the British royal family.

Debbie Harry was the lead singer of the band Blondie. She is still performing as a solo artist today.

Rise and fall

Blondie was a U.S. **New Wave** band. Blondie had played at CBGB for several years, and the albums it released in 1976 and 1977 were noticed around the world.

However, things were not going so well for Patti Smith. At a concert in 1977, Patti fell off the stage headfirst onto a concrete floor. She broke her neck, her sight was damaged, and her legs were partly paralyzed. However, only weeks later, she was performing again, wearing a neck brace.

Sid Vicious

John Ritchie earned the nickname Sid Vicious after he was bitten by Johnny Rotten's hamster, Sid. He was not a natural musician, but he taught himself to play bass guitar by listening to a Ramones album. Sadly, he became a heroin **addict** and was only 21 when he died.

Punk Fashion

Punk music wanted to rebel against **commercial pop** and **disco** music. Punk fashion was also designed to challenge normal ideas. In the United Kingdom, Malcolm McLaren and Vivienne Westwood had a huge influence on punk fashion. Their store in London sold a range of shocking designer clothes that were often torn and had zippers, studs, and safety pins added. They often used materials such as plastic, leather, and plaid wool. The clothes were expensive, but punk fans were encouraged to make their own clothes if they could not afford "a tailor-made **vinyl** outfit."

Vivienne Westwood

Vivienne Westwood studied art and taught in an elementary school before she met Malcolm McLaren. In 1971 they opened their first clothing store together and began selling her designs. The Sex Pistols made her clothes famous, and they formed a key part of the punk look.

Vivienne Westwood (left) is still designing striking and unusual fashion today.

Make your own punk outfit

Why not try what Malcolm McLaren suggested and make your own punk outfit?

You will need:

- old, worn-out clothes, especially anything denim or plaid. Do not use clothes that can still be worn, since you could donate them to a charity shop.
- safety pins
- face paints.

Steps to follow:

1. Look at pictures of punk clothes and makeup in this book.

2. Work with a partner. Decide who will be the model and who will be the designer.

3. Decide what item of clothing you want to make. Do you want a dress or just a top or pants?

4. Cut up the old clothes to make wide strips of fabric. Use the safety pins to hold the material together on the model. You may have to rip or cut the strips of fabric into smaller sections. Experiment with the style.

5. Use face paints to give the model punk makeup. Look at pages 16 and 17 to get some ideas.

6. Take a photo of your creation.

Ramones style

U.S. musicians such as The Ramones and Patti Smith often wore leather jackets, T-shirts, torn jeans, and sneakers. In the mid-1970s, these clothes could be shocking to ordinary people. It was a simple style that reflected punk's short, basic songs. It was also a look that fans could easily copy. Often people wrote on their T-shirts to make a statement.

Punk slogans

People did not just wear T-shirts with **slogans**. Badges were another important part of punk style that people could buy or make for themselves. Often these badges had the name of a band on them, or song **lyrics**. Other badges had **anarchy** symbols or slogans that were designed to shock.

The Mohawk hairstyle was named after the Native American Mohawk people. It took a lot of time to style and maintain!

Hairstyles

Punk hair could be different styles. The Ramones and other early U.S. punk bands tended to have long hair. In the United Kingdom, punk hair was often dyed bright colors such as green, pink, orange, or red. It was meant to look as unnatural as possible, and punks used glue or hairspray to hold their hair in stiff styles. The Mohawk was a famous style, with both sides of the head shaved and a stiff strip of hair sticking up in the middle. Other punk hair was spiked or left looking shaggy and wild.

Punk makeup

Makeup was another simple way to make people look rebellious and shocking. Punk makeup was easy for male and female fans to copy and often included heavy black eyeliner. Black or bright red lipstick and very pale skin completed the unnatural look. Some punks even applied warpaint in bright stripes on their faces.

Many older people found punk makeup very shocking at first. Today, we are used to seeing unusual styles.

Punk Art

Like punk music and fashion, punk art had a "do it yourself" look. In the 1970s, music was recorded onto large, flat **vinyl** records. Many punk records had very striking covers. Some famous album covers had lettering that looked as if it had been ripped out of newspapers and magazines and stuck on the record. This kind of writing reminded people of kidnappers' notes and made the punk bands seem like outlaws.

Fanzines and flyers

Fanzines were a big part of the punk **subculture**. Like album covers, fanzines also had ripped-out lettering and images from newspapers pasted in and often **defaced**. This was before the time of home computers, so text was often handwritten. The fanzines and flyers advertising concerts were usually photocopied in black and white and then given to the few people who were in the know. This gave the subculture a secret, underground feel that was very appealing to fans.

The Sex Pistols' record covers famously used ripped-out lettering from newspapers and looked very rough.

The Ramones' logo

The Ramones' band logo was created by the artist Arturo Vega. He had already made T-shirts for the band when he decided to create a logo based on the **U.S. Presidential Seal**. He chose this symbol because he saw the band as an alternative "all-American" institution. He put the Ramones' **lyrics** "Hey ho let's go" on the scroll in the eagle's beak. Later, he added a baseball bat because Johnny Ramone was a fan of the game .

The Ramones displayed their logo onstage, so it became a key part of their identity.

Punk Politics

Pop music had started in the 1950s with rock and roll. Musicians such as Elvis Presley and The Beatles had brought great changes to the music scene, making new sounds popular with young people. In the years after World War II, there was an optimistic feeling that was reflected in upbeat pop tunes. By the 1970s, however, music had become an **industry** led by businesspeople rather than musicians. Large record companies and musicians earned lots of money and lived very differently from the ordinary young people their music was meant to be for.

"I hate Pink Floyd"

By the 1970s, life in many countries was hard for young people, and they found it difficult to get jobs. Young **working-class** people wanted their own sound and attitude in order to rebel against accepted **conventions** and limits. Johnny Rotten was spotted wearing a T-shirt with the popular band Pink Floyd written on it. Rotten had written the words "I hate" above the band name. This was his way of rejecting the accepted music of the time.

In the United States in the 1970s, people showed their opposition to the government by demonstrating against the Vietnam War.

The anarchy symbol is sometimes seen drawn on walls as an expression of rebellion.

Music with a message?

Punk music did not have one single message, other than the idea of rebelling against restrictions in society. Some British bands, such as The Clash, were political, protesting about racism and the problems that working-class people faced. Some punk bands sang about **anarchy**. Anarchy is a situation in which there is no law and order and government has no control. Punks wanted to shock.

Punk's Aftermath

In 1978 The Sex Pistols visited the United States. The tour was a disaster. Sid Vicious was a drug **addict** and was unable to perform well. At the end of the tour, Johnny Rotten and Sid Vicious were fired from the band. The Sex Pistols were finished.

Punk moves on

From this time on, things started to change. The shocking edge that the first punk bands brought to youth **culture** had gone. Many imitation bands made the punk sound more **conventional**. For the remaining original bands, it became harder to perform in the United Kingdom, since punk bands were banned in many places. Many musicians, such as Patti Smith, were tired of punks being violent and behaving badly in other ways.

For many people, Sid Vicious will always be the face of punk music.

Death of punk?

In 1978 Sid Vicious's girlfriend, Nancy Spungen, was murdered in a hotel room in New York City. Sid died from a drug overdose just a few months later. By the start of the 1980s, punk rock was just one of many musical **subcultures**. People began to have more money and there was less to rebel against. Punk became something of a joke and was rejected by young people who were looking for something new.

Punk around the world

Punk took off around the world. Die Toten Hosen was a German band. The name literally means "The Dead Trousers," but it also means "boring." Australian punk bands such as The Saints were popular during the 1970s. Punk rock took off in Japan in the early 1980s, with bands such as The Star Club and Friction.

Young people in Japan also adopted the punk look and attitude.

Punk's Influence

By the late 1970s, some early punk bands had become more mainstream and popular. Blondie became very big and its **pop** album, *Parallel Lines*, was an international hit in 1978. Other bands that had been around for years, such as Talking Heads, moved on from punk and found new audiences.

The influence of punk was seen in popular 1980s bands such as The Cure, who wore wild makeup and hairstyles; The Pretenders, whose lead singer had worked for Malcolm McLaren; and Adam and the Ants, who wore warpaint. But while new electronic sounds were taking over the music scene, U.S. punk bands, such as Black Flag, were making angry, political music again. The 1990s saw **grunge** music becoming popular with bands such as Nirvana, Soundgarden, and Pearl Jam.

Nirvana and other grunge bands were heavily influenced by punk, with a raw, noisy sound and angry **lyrics**.

Make your own punk song

Punk songs were typically short, loud, and fast. The words were often shouted instead of sung. Classic punk lyrics were often very simple and direct and were repeated several times in a song. Try taking The Ramones song "I Don't Care" and write your own words.

Steps to follow:

1. If you can, listen to "I Don't Care" by The Ramones on a CD or on the Internet.

2. This Ramones song repeats the words "I don't care" three times, followed by the words "About this world." In your song, repeat "I don't care" in the same way but then choose your own fourth line. You don't have to really mean what you write and you could make it funny if you like! For example, you could write, "I don't care / About eating cheese."

3. Repeat the words "I don't care" again and then choose another line beginning "About ..." Try to make it rhyme with the previous line. For example, you could write, "I don't care / About eating peas."

4. Repeat step 3 and finish with "I don't care."

5. Try performing your song with punk attitude!

Punk today

Many musicians playing today have a punk look or sound. Other types of music and style have taken over from punk. "Emo" bands, such as Fall Out Boy, Panic! at the Disco, and Funeral for a Friend, and their fans wear unusual clothes and makeup. Their song lyrics often describe how they feel like outsiders in the **conventional** world.

Punk goes pop

Many mainstream pop musicians owe a lot to punk. Singers such as Pink, Lady Gaga, and Gwen Stefani have a classic punk look. Pop bands such as McFly and Good Charlotte have a spiky-haired punk style, but they are not rebels. Instead they play safe pop tunes and perform for charities and on movie soundtracks.

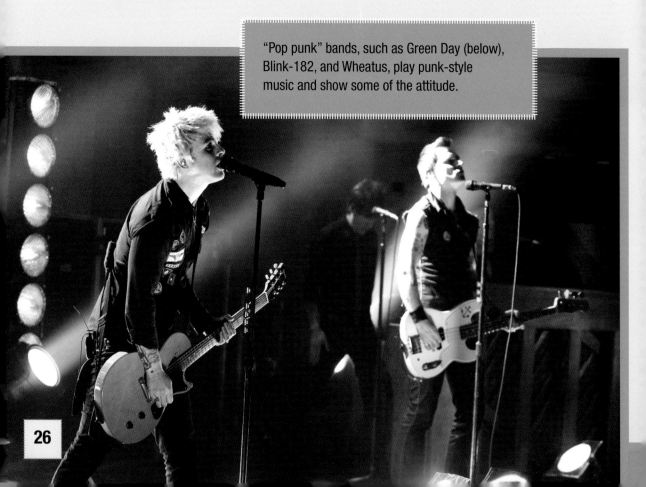

"Pop punk" bands, such as Green Day (below), Blink-182, and Wheatus, play punk-style music and show some of the attitude.

Still rocking today

Many musicians from the early days of punk are still performing today. Their music has changed over the years, but The Pretenders, Blondie, The Buzzcocks, Elvis Costello, The Damned, Iggy Pop, and Bad Religion are still as popular today as ever.

Punk's future

Punk music, fashions, and hairstyles do not shock many people today. Even the tamest boy bands have spiky hair and play loud, fast guitars. Television shows such as *American Idol* make singers famous for performing new versions of old songs that appeal to as many people as possible. Do people have anything to rebel against today? Are our lives too comfortable? Maybe in the future musicians will become angry again and find a new way to shock the system. What do you think?

Artists such as Pink owe their look to punk. But will singers of the future rebel against the music **industry** as punk musicians did in the past?

Timeline

1969	Detroit bands such as MC5 and The Stooges hit the music scene
1971	The band The New York Dolls forms in New York City
	The term "punk rock" is first used
1972	Malcolm McLaren visits New York City and hears the new punk sounds
1973	The CBGB club in New York City starts hosting bands such as The Ramones
	The band Television forms
1974	The Saints form in Australia
1975	The New York Dolls split up
	The Sex Pistols perform their first concert
	Patti Smith releases the album *Horses* and becomes "the Godmother of Punk"
	The Vietnam War ends
1976	*Punk* magazine starts in New York City
	The Sex Pistols become famous for the chaos at their concerts. They release their first album and gain a bad reputation on British television.
	The Ramones release the album *The Ramones*
	The bands Siouxsie and the Banshees and The Clash form
1977	The Sex Pistols are dumped by their **record label** and Sid Vicious joins the band

1978	The Sex Pistols tour the United States
	Nancy Spungen, the girlfriend of Sid Vicious, is murdered in a New York City hotel room
1979	Sid Vicious dies of a drug overdose
1987	The band Nirvana forms
	Grunge music becomes popular
	The band Green Day forms in California
1995	The band Wheatus forms in New York
	Gwen Stefani and her band No Doubt hit the big time
2000	The singer Pink releases her first record
2001	Emo/**pop** punk band Fall Out Boy starts playing in the Chicago area
	The band Funeral for a Friend forms in Wales, in the United Kingdom
2004	The band Panic! at the Disco forms in Las Vegas, Nevada
	The pop band McFly becomes famous
2008	Lady Gaga releases her first album, *The Fame*
2009	Johnny Rotten's band Public Image Limited starts to play live again for the first time in 17 years
2010	Malcolm McLaren's family asks people to have a "moment of mayhem", instead of a moment of silence, to mark his death

Glossary

addict person who has become dependent on a substance such as alcohol or drugs

anarchy situation in which there is no law and order and government has no control

authorities lawmakers and enforcers, such as government and police

chord musical sound made by playing several notes together

commercial to do with making money

conservative traditional and against change

controversial issue that divides opinion

conventional accepted way of doing something

culture ideas and beliefs of a group of people

deface damage or spoil on purpose

disco type of dance music that started in the 1970s

fanzine type of homemade magazine made by fans for other fans

generation group of people born at around the same time

grunge style of music that started in the 1980s. It was partly inspired by punk and is played using electric guitars.

industry business

lyrics words to a song

media sources of news, such as newspapers, radio, and television

New Wave type of music that started in the late 1970s. It was not as hard as punk and included more electronic sounds.

notorious well known for bad behavior

pop popular; a type of music and dancing originally supported by young people

record label company that makes and sells music records

slogan easily remembered phrase

subculture separate group with its own beliefs and ideas within a larger culture

U.S. Presidential Seal image or coat of arms that represents the U.S. president

vinyl type of plastic material. Punk music was released on vinyl records.

working class people who work in certain jobs, including manual labor such as construction work, and their families

Find Out More

Books

Doeden, Matt. *Green Day: Keeping Their Edge* (Gateway Biography series). Minneapolis: Lerner, 2007.

Masar, Brenden. *The History of Punk Rock* (Music Library series). Farmington Hills, Mich.: Lucent, 2006.

Schaefer, A. R. *Forming a Band* (Rock Music Library series). North Mankato, Minn.: Capstone, 2004.

Websites

http://rockhall.com
The Rock and Roll Hall of Fame Museum website has information on many important punk bands, including The Ramones, The Clash, The Sex Pistols, Patti Smith, and The Stooges. Use the search field to find out more about these different bands.

www.britishmusicexperience.com/index.cfm?PageID=50
The British Music Experience Museum has an exhibition that looks at the music scene in the United Kingdom from 1977 to 1985. It also has pages about The Sex Pistols, Siouxsie and the Banshees, The Damned, and The Buzzcocks.

Place to visit

Rock and Roll Hall of Fame and Museum
1100 Rock and Roll Boulevard
Cleveland, Ohio 44114
Tel: (216) 781-7625
http://rockhall.com

Index